SHE IS KING

Giovanni Thompson

Copyright © Giovanni Thompson, 2021
Cover image: © Chocolate Readings
Published by Chocolate Readings
www.chocolatereadings.com
ISBN-13: 978-1-7366962-2-4

Publisher's Note
Printed and bound in the United States of America. All rights reserved. No part of this book may be reproduced or transmitted in any form or by any means, electronic or mechanical, including photocopying, recording, or by any information storage and retrieval system except by a reviewer who may quote brief passages in a review to be printed in a magazine, newspaper, or on the Web without permission in writing from **Giovanni Thompson**.

Although the author and publisher have made every effort to ensure the accuracy and completeness of information contained in this book, we assume no responsibility for errors, inaccuracies, omissions, or any inconsistency herein. The advice and strategies contained herein may not be suitable for your situation. You should consult with a professional where appropriate. Neither the publisher nor the author shall be liable for damages arising from here.

DEDICATION

This piece of myself is dedicated to my children Javon, Jovani, Parker & Brave. You have pushed me to strive for greatness. I hope that you grasp the best of me.

This book is specifically dedicated to my grandfather. You are the greatest man I ever met. I'm grateful for everything you taught me. Thank you Pop.

Giovanni

She Is King

CONTENTS

Introduction	7
QUARTER ONE	**9**
Allow Me To Introduce Myself	11
Model Behavior	21
Goodbye Model, Hello Styling	31
Being A Woman In A Male-Dominated Industry	35
It Wasn't *All* Bad	45
Know Thy Self	49
QUARTER TWO	**53**
Having A Seat At The Table	55
Empowerment Is Essential	61
Ladies, Use Your Voice	67
QUARTER THREE	**71**
Learning To Love Giovanni	73
I'm A Baby Mom… And?	79
Balancing It All	84
QUARTER FOUR	**89**
Becoming A Boss	91
She Owns A What?	97
Everyone Can't Go… And That's Okay	105
Please Hold The Applause	109
OVERTIME	**115**
Lessons to Becoming A Leader	117
About the Author	*123*

She Is King

INTRODUCTION

I grew up believing I could do or be anything. I watched my parents level up time after time. They took risks that others wouldn't, helped many, and handled their business. I never knew how watching them would help me more than any school would ever do. To contrary belief, I never went to college; you will read why. With them as my first set of mentors, I never really had to.

The hustle and understanding of how to maneuver in different arenas come from the grind. It also comes from trials and errors.

The mistakes you encounter to get to the top should be the same reason why you never hit the bottom if you are smart. My parents, as husband and wife, were able to do amazing things together. In contrast, I am single Black mom who got pregnant at an early age; I've had to fight through the stereotypes and boundaries alone. In the past twelve years, I've fought for myself and others. Understanding God's grace, I will never feel worthy to say I've earned anything. But babyyyyyy, let me tell you: I can call myself "King" with confidence...

Keep reading, and you will see why *She is King...*

She Is King

Allow Me To Introduce Myself

She Is King

By now, I would say you've either known me, heard of me, seen me, or have seen my work somewhere. I've always prided myself on being the most capable but not the most visible. With each accomplishment and glass ceiling I break, I realized that being in the spotlight is inevitable at this point. Bear with me...

Before I was a mom of four and an entrepreneur, I was a pretty laid-back young lady who did the typical things young ladies do — I went to the mall with my friends, played basketball, you know, just lived a regular, suburban life. I wasn't too wild or anything, but you know, like many teen girls, I had my eyes on the boys. One cutie ended up getting my undivided attention, and um, well, in my freshman year of high school, I got pregnant for the star football player. I can still recall the day I found out vividly. My dad took me to the gynecologist for a routine checkup. And lo and behold, the doctor tells my dad that I was pregnant. I was mortified! And that was just the beginning of the shame and embarrassment I would feel. I wasn't the only one feeling this way, either.

Unfortunately, my dad had called the entire family on our way home; therefore, when I got home, all my family members were sitting there, waiting for me. They all asked me the same questions, "Why did you do it?" "What were you thinking?" You know, the typical questions that should be rhetorical because I mean, how do you really answer those types of questions in front of your family? I can't tell them the reason I had sex was that I was obsessed with the most popular senior in high school. No answer would have been good enough anyway, so I played dumb.

At that time, my parents were divorced, and my mom lived in North Carolina. It was hard dealing with the initial shock of it all without my mother being there, but I got through it.

Lord knows I didn't want to tell my mom. I wished my dad would do it for me, but I knew that wouldn't happen. I remember the night before I went to my mom's, my dad had a breakdown. He cried and held me extremely tight. He was praying so loud. It shook me. I could tell that he was just completely overwhelmed with the whole situation. He really couldn't handle it emotionally. I had disappointed him beyond belief, and my mother was next.

Let me tell you: that was the longest one hour and forty minutes of my life! I cried the entire time from Philadelphia to Charlotte. I had everyone on that plane feeling sorry for me, too. The flight attendants were consoling me as best as they could. Hey, what else do you expect a

14-year-old to do? I was in shambles until I got in front of my mom. I was expecting part two of my experience in New Jersey, but I got the total opposite. I thought my mom was going to go crazy on me, but she didn't. When I got off the plane, she met me with open arms. She went above and beyond as a parent dealing with that type of situation. As peaceful as my spirit was, my conscience wouldn't let me rest. At the end of the day, I'm still a young girl in the ninth grade, having a baby soon. This was nothing to be happy about.

Needless to say, no one celebrated this achievement. To be honest, I understand why. While being pregnant is beautiful, for me, it was a horrific experience. I wasn't in a relationship with the child's father, and he didn't want to have anything to do with me or the baby. His family made such a big deal about everything and even went as far as saying it wasn't his baby just to protect him and his career. I got pregnant the first time I had sex, so that was a total lie. The truth of the matter is, I didn't want to be pregnant either. However, my parents made it clear that abortion was not an option. I was terrified and kind of upset with myself. At the time of the incident, I was living with my father. However, things got so crazy. My dad eventually sent me to my mom's because he just couldn't handle the situation. I mean, I couldn't handle the situation, and it was mine! So, I was relieved when he sent me. (Well, eventually, I was relieved; initially, I was beyond scared.)

So, after things got real, my pregnant belly and I left New Jersey and went down south to go live with my mom in North Carolina. That's when the reality of me being pregnant set in. They enrolled me in a school for pregnant girls to stay on track with my grades. I mean, it was okay, I guess. Everything was going as normal as possible until the night my pregnancy took a turn for the worst. I remember being in so much pain as the ambulance arrived. When we got to the hospital, I only remember my mom being outside, out the curtain, sobbing uncontrollably.

I had to deliver my baby, knowing he wouldn't survive.

As if being a 14-year-old pregnant girl wasn't traumatic enough, delivering a baby that I couldn't keep pushed me over the edge. It was like it all happened so fast. One day I was pregnant, and the next, I wasn't. That was hard for me to accept and understand. I thought about how quickly my life changed, yet again. Everything was going fine until one day I just wasn't feeling well. I remember complaining to my mom that I had stomach pains. We went to the hospital with a feeling of optimism; we never thought the outcome would be horrific. After checking my cervix, they informed us that I had to deliver the baby. They said there wasn't anything they could do to stop the contractions. They also mentioned that the baby was too young for them to even try to save it. So, at just 24 weeks, I was forced to deliver my baby: A baby that I'd never get to hold, love or raise. That broke my young spirit. My mother did such an amazing job, helping me to prepare to be a young mother. We were kinda at the point of accepting our new life. So, when this happened, it hurt so much that I didn't talk for months.

People are always shocked when I say that, but it's true. I didn't have anything to say. So much pain was weighing my young soul down, and I didn't know how to articulate it. There I was, basically still a baby myself, delivering a baby. I still felt abandoned by my father for forcing me to move in with my mother. Not to mention, the pain from their divorce was still present. It was hidden, but it was there. So yeah, the entire experience traumatized me on a level I can't explain.

Eventually, I learned to accept my experience for what it was and take the first step to heal. I was so confused; I didn't understand anything that was happening. Even after such a traumatic experience, I still had to leave my mom again. I ended up moving back to New Jersey about six months after that experience, back to my old life with my dad. My next few years of high school were spent running the streets and hanging out. My grades were always up to par, though.

And then, I got pregnant again. Are you judging me? Don't judge me. Thanks. I haven't let my children be an excuse for not pursuing my goals. And to be honest, I don't know if that's always a good thing. We'll talk about that in another chapter.

So, as I mentioned earlier, I have four kids now. I gave birth to my first son at 18. And again, it wasn't anything I wanted to celebrate per se. I'm not ashamed of my son at all; I just wasn't ready or prepared. College was in my near future, so that was what I was preparing for. I found out about my pregnancy after I graduated from high school. I was a little disappointed because I had just received a full scholarship to attend Baylor University in Texas. Initially, I was going to attend, pregnant and all. They were still going to accept me, but then I started getting really sick. I started throwing up uncontrollably, and I lost over thirty pounds in a few weeks. I ended up getting a PICC line and TPN. I was on IVs at home, the whole nine months. I had something called hyperemesis gravidarum. Once it got to that point, my parents said, "There's no way that you're going to college." I was scheduled to leave sometime in August, but I found out I was pregnant in June. All that stuff happened in a matter of those two months. Therefore, we decided as a family that I should stay home and give birth to my son. In a way, I felt it all happened for a reason because, in October, my brother got hurt, and I was around to help as much as possible. To be completely transparent, I wasn't so upset about not going to college. I realized that my life's goals needed to shift now that I was a mom, and that's exactly what happened.

After I had my son, I got interested in the fashion and entertainment industry. When I wasn't helping my brother, I thought of what I wanted to do with my life. I did my research and fell in love with the behind-the-scenes stuff. Once I felt confident enough to get my foot in the door, I went for it. Eventually, I went to New York for a while and worked as a model. My parents kept my baby so that I could start my journey — and that's exactly what I did.

I went to New York and thought I was about to be famous. But chileeeee...

She Is King

Model Behavior

She Is King

Most people are unaware that I used to model, but yep, that's how I jumped into the industry. I became interested in fashion as a young girl. My mom was always fly back in the day, so it was easy to be influenced by fashion designers and creatives. Watching my mother show her interest in fashion kind of sparked mine. My parents had their own custom clothier business back in the day. My mom and I started designing things together, and the next thing I know, people are telling me that I should model. At first, I was unsure. I found myself toying with the idea of being on somebody's runway trying to model. Eventually, I gave in to the idea and started doing my thing.

    I started doing little stuff locally. And then, two of my very good friends, Ryan B. and Tony, moved to New York. I couldn't wait for them to get settled so I could get in the mix. If I wanted to take this modeling thing seriously, I would have to leave New Jersey and head to New York, so I did. By the way, Ryan went on to be a world-renown hairstylist, makeup artist, and beauty expert for Vogue and Nars, and Tony was a designer for Ralph Lauren, for like, forever.

Leaving New Jersey to pursue my modeling career was not an easy decision. Remember, I'm a mother of a toddler. Can I do this? I had my doubts and reconsidered my decision over and over (and over). Finally, after getting enough support from my parents, I decided to leap.

Modeling opened up a whole new world for me; I had some of the best experiences ever. Going to Fashion Week and all those dope fashion events was heaven to me. I wasn't used to all the backstage shenanigans; that took some getting used to. Once I found my lane, I stayed in it. I wasn't trying to step on any toes or get caught up in the industry norm like drugs, eating disorders, etc. Because of some of the things I saw backstage early in my career, I still don't drink or use drugs to this day. I really focused on learning the industry so I could try different things. I'm glad I did that because eventually, I determined that modeling just ain't for me.

I wasn't in the legal drinking age, and I had no clue about life at all. I really had no clue about what I was getting into. I had other model friends at the time. Some are now famous, while others are stay-at-home moms. They were more experienced but still lacked enough knowledge to avoid the pitfalls of the fashion industry. And I was no exception. While there are different dark and negative things a young model can experience, I'm grateful that it is not my story. I did find myself in some pretty uncomfortable situations that had me second-guessing my decision to model and the industry in general.

As a model, I dealt with a lot of scrutiny on casting calls. I was about 120 pounds, and I still wasn't skinny enough. If I'd lost any more weight, I would have been a skeleton. The pressure to fit it and look like the other models started to get to me. I mean, if I don't look the part or can't fit the clothes, I can't model. If I can't model, I can't make money. And no money means I have to go back to New Jersey. Back in my day, you had to be sample size to get booked. NO EXCEPTIONS!

I was so discouraged. I had my heart set on being a successful model, but apparently, I was not model material. Dealing with that type of scrutiny was the first time I realized what the world really is. I really got into the vanity of the world, like, you know stuff really was about and so, um, you know.

I would go to casting calls and fittings, excited, waiting for my agent. Only for me to hear, "Oh, you didn't book this job because your body is looking too urban." I would be so heartbroken. Like, what the freak does that even mean? Too urban? Or I'd hear, "You need to lose more weight," you know, condescending stuff like that. I was already skinny enough, so I wasn't sure what else they wanted me to do. If I only had a dollar for every time that I heard, "Giovonni if you don't lose weight, you won't work."

Facing all those rejections challenged me to just keep going and trying to prove them wrong, even though I wasn't always able to do it. However, it built this new level of strength inside of me. Experiencing criticism, adversity, and sometimes racism truly helped me become stronger rather than hindering me.

After many more of those experiences, it was the last one that took me completely out of the game as a model. I went for a casting call for a very famous undergarment brand. As I went in there, ready to do my thing, the casting director pulled his penis out. I was confused, shocked, and a little worried. I didn't know this man or what he was capable of. I just stood there, waiting to see what he'd say or do next. He gave me an ultimatum.

I was horrified as I listened to his bribe. "You know, you want the job," he said, looking and sounding like a creep. All I could think of was all the other girls he's done this to. He ran his mouth about how important being a part of the campaign would be, especially for a Black girl. Yep, he went there. I was done after that. I remember walking out of there and standing on the corner in Manhattan, bawling my eyes out. Once I caught my breath and calmed myself down, I called my mom and said, "All right, I'm done. I'm coming home." By the way, that campaign was one of their biggest campaigns to date. I got sick to my stomach every time the commercial came on TV, or I saw it in a magazine.

Being behind the scenes increased my work ethic. When you are responsible for how things work, you have no option other than to stay on your toes for being the go-to person for an event, music video, or tour. I became a beast. My reputation preceded me in every room I walked in. I was making a name for myself, especially with the artists. My goal is always excellence. I make it my duty to push the envelope on every aspect. People started hiring me for the "Gio Global Way." I was often told, "You shouldn't do it that way," or "Why are you doing all that?" I did all that because that's what I wanted to do! I told myself over a decade ago that whenever I do something, it has to be BIG, it has to be different, it has to be me. My favorite Jay-Z line is, "I rather die enormous than live dormant, that's how we on it!" I've rehearsed that verse in my head many times. I really live by it.

If you take anything from this book, please remember DO NOT LET PEOPLE TRICK YOU OUT YOUR SPOT.

People will try and deter you from what you want to do for many reasons. Sometimes they are fueled by fear. Sometimes they are driven by lack of vision, and sometimes is just plain ol' hatin'. Whatever it is, ignore it. Stick to the script, meaning stick to YOUR plan.

Every time I transitioned to a different industry, whether fashion, music, or sports, I made sure I entered as myself— nothing more, nothing less. Fashion helped me to establish what I wanted and what I didn't want.

The music industry helped me to express what I wanted and stand on who I was becoming.

The sports industry has helped to be able to help others become who they dream of being. Being true to myself has taken me into different arenas...
Literally.

She Is King

Goodbye Model, Hello Styling

She Is King

Although I really wanted to make my modeling career work, I knew that it wasn't for me. I wasn't in the business of selling myself for a gig. I also didn't want to force myself to be a size 0 or whatever size they expected of me. It was way too much pressure, and I wasn't happy anymore. So, when I went home to New Jersey, I didn't get stagnant to my son, though. When I wasn't being a mom, I was planning my next endeavor. It was almost like my drive and ambition went into overdrive when I left New York. Since I still wasn't sure of what I wanted to do, I started helping my mom out with her designs and her shows. A new passion for styling was starting to form.

I fell in love and ended up having another baby. And nope, that didn't slow me down or stop me. In fact, it gave me, even more drive to follow the goals I set for myself.

Once in the swing of being a mother of two, I started transitioning more into the fashion and styling aspect of the industry: I absolutely loved it.

Being a stylist helped me to use my natural creativity. I started exploring different looks, and that set me apart from the other stylists in my era. I already had the relationships with the designers from when I was a model, so it was cool. Eventually, I transitioned into doing something behind the camera work, creative directing, and project management. But it wasn't an easy transition. Here's how it went down...

Being A Woman In A Male-Dominated Industry

She Is King

The popular James Brown song says that this is a man's world. It also goes on to say that it's nothing without a woman or a girl, and I think they hate that! It shows how women are treated in professional settings. With the way I carried myself in both industries, I saw quickly that earned respect turned into competition once I started progressing into elevated positions. In the beginning, I was tested and had to prove that I was not the one to play with. But who wants to do all of that? Women shouldn't have to prove themselves emotionally, though. Allow us to adapt and do our thing naturally.

Okay, let me back up.

If you plan to work in a male-dominated industry, understand that they'll test you from the beginning to see how far you can go. It starts with the comments, sexual comments, of course; you know, trying to gauge you. Then once you've surpassed them on the ladder of success, the comments get disrespectful. I observed that as I climbed that ladder; most men kept their distance from me. I was now a woman in power, and they didn't know how to communicate the admiration.

For whatever reason, most men have a problem with respecting a woman in position. Moreover, they always put themselves above you even if your title says otherwise. It's always an underlying thing there. And so, I had to learn quickly to develop boundaries and stick to them.

When I was at the label, I always said it was like being thrown into the water with sharks. I was the only female in A&R during that time which meant that I had to adapt immediately. I cannot tell you how many times I would go on the road, be backstage, or even in meetings where people would think that I'm the artist's girlfriend, which was the complete opposite of who I truly was. After they make their wrong assumption, I'd explain that I'm the person working on the project, or I'm one that sent them the email. I would say to them, "I'm Giovonni who sent you the email," and in response, they would say, "I thought Giovonni was a guy." Unfortunately, I'd get it all the time, but I realized that it was because of how I dressed.

Sigh.

Once I realized this, I started showing up to work and meetings in sweatpants, tights, and the latest sneakers. And you know, wearing sneakers and sweats wasn't always my thing. Coming from the fashion industry, I was always fashionable, but it wasn't working for me in that environment.

So, I had to pivot to slow down so much nonsense; I had to toughen up. At first, I hated having to do that, but in hindsight, I needed to. So yeah, once I got my footing, and I felt like I knew who I was and what I was doing, I started barking back. If somebody assumed I was someone else, I would ask, "Are you dumb or something?" I got to the point where I told myself, "I'm not doing this with any of them." To keep your sanity in a male-dominated field, I suggest you do the same because they know exactly who you are a lot of times. They're just testing you, and I didn't have time for that.

After that side of me emerged, things got real when I felt disrespected. I've gotten into a couple of fights with men at meetings.

Yep, read it again.

How many times did you read it?

I know that's hard to envision, but it's true.

I've had fights with men because they'd say something out of pocket or call me a name, and I would snap. I've thrown my iPad across the room in meetings when somebody said something crazy to me. I know you're reading this thinking, "Was it really that serious?" Well, yeah. It was because if I didn't do it, they would have thought it was okay to keep disrespecting me. It became known that I didn't have a problem being that person. Just imagine the frustration in an office setting where people constantly want to disrespect you, especially when you're just trying to do your job and change the game.

After all, I noticed that some of the younger women were watching me. I definitely didn't want them to think that they'd have to put up with crap just to keep their position and be in the mix. I wanted them to know that it's okay to speak up for themselves with authority. Men won't like that, and that's okay, too. I made sure that I was very clear about that with the young girls that were around me. So, you know, I've gotten into some scuffles, and it's only because of all testing that goes on at certain levels. And if you test me, pop quiz, I am going to pop you, period, lol. But on a serious note, if you find yourself in a situation where a man in power is giving you a proposition, I suggest that you quickly nip it in the bud.

Listen, you do not need to use anything other than your gifts and talents to get ahead. You don't need to use your sensuality to be successful — that's what your brain is for. No shade, just being honest. It amazes me when I think about all the things that I've been able to accomplish independently without a man's hands. You have the power, the skills, and the talent to do the same.

If you have morals, don't compromise them. If you have integrity, don't compromise it. Do not question your self-worth. When it comes to your self-respect, compromising is not an option.

You know, one of the things that I had to consider is the salacious comments and rumors that will be told about me. I had to prep myself for the invasive questions: Is that your natural body? Oh, are you sleeping with this person? Unfortunately, I've already gotten accused of sleeping with some of my players and clients — but, like why?

No disrespect, but why would I sleep with somebody I'm paying?

Okay, let me bring it back.

I work hard to clear the path for the girls and women who are behind me or by my side. You know, many women don't have the confidence to move in their authenticity. I would like to change that. Well, at least try anyway.

I remember when I had started an athletic sportswear company. I thought this would be a fun and exciting venture. I was ready to go into meetings, share my ideas, contribute to the creative process, you know, do my thing. Well, that ain't how it went down at all! I shouldn't have been so shocked that things went completely left. The board of investors and athletic directors were, of course, all men. Men who didn't hesitate to let me know how they felt about a woman having a seat at their table. They tried to make me feel like I was just a piece of meat, treating me as if I were there to take notes rather than give them. I felt unheard, and it became a strain trying to get this project off the ground. It got to the point that I became intimidated to be around the other investors by myself.

I never went to a meeting by myself. I already knew what was up, and I wasn't going to play that game. So, to keep me from that kind of condescending energy, my partner was at every meeting that we had with any athletic director. This was to show that I would not contend with sexual harassment or stereotypic treatments. I was the lead partner in the company.

However, it didn't matter at that time because to men, I was just a woman. So, my input didn't matter, and my thoughts were invalid. I couldn't stand that. And you know what I really can't stand?

That has not very much changed today.

It's because of how men treat women in these male-dominated industries that society's perspective on femininity is what it is. We can't even dress however we want because some man, somewhere, has something to say. A huge part of me wants to encourage women to wear whatever the hell they want. But the part of me that knows better has to be honest. While I love to see women rocking cute heels and fly dresses, however, to avoid having to defend your career or reputation, it's best to dress it down and use your intelligence to exude your femininity, at least in the office environments. There's always a time and place to get fly; just keep it to a minimum to avoid being harassed or labeled. I found that last longer for sure.

Now, ladies, don't feel like just because I suggest not dressing up in male-dominated industries mean that you are being controlled. It's about playing chess, not checkers. If you truly have passion for the work that you do, then play the game to win. I hate that our clothes, bodies, and essence as women trigger sexual in men. However, we can't let that distract us from the common goal. We can't let the things they say or do to us slide, i.e., being called the "B" word.

You know, men wear me out. They'll push all the buttons a woman has that puts her in B mode, and then they're surprised when she pops off. Like, why? And if we're not the B-word, then we're so mean. Really? Are women mean? Or are we not in the mood for your disrespect? I mean, let me know.

I laugh when I think of this, but a couple of people in the industry call me "Suge Knight." I'm not that bad. I'm a very kind-hearted person, but I'm not about to let anyone get at me crazy, especially when it comes to my business.

IT WASN'T <u>ALL</u> BAD

Yes, I had some difficult times working in a predominantly male environment. However, when I reflect on my experiences, some of my best lessons were learned in the most negative situations. One of the best lessons that I've learned working with men is not to second-guess myself. I don't have to dumb down myself to be heard or fidget when I'm in rooms with people who aren't as knowledgeable as I am. I would never do that again.

It took me a while to operate at my full potential because I thought someone would tell me to chill and stop overpowering others. After my partner and I went separate ways, I had no choice but to step up and go harder. To be honest, operating to my full potential scared me a little. I didn't want to run my business or launch a project by myself. I wanted to have people around, but one day, I had a conversation with my mom, who reminded me to focus on the vision and not the people. She said, "There are many moving parts to the vision. There are different puzzle pieces, and they'll get moved out until you find the right fit." And so, after that realization, I stopped being upset about my past experiences and used those tough lessons to propel me into my current role.

Know Thy Self

She Is King

Before you take on a role in a male-dominated industry, I definitely recommend having a plan of action. First, build your fortitude up. Build your confidence. Don't be surprised by the unprofessionalism you'll encounter. Prepare yourself for the unthinkable so that you can respond and react in a way that will honor your womanhood when things go down. It'll be tempting not to put a man in his place when he disrespects you, but do what you need to do, professionally, of course. This way, the other men in the office or on the team won't try you.

Make sure that you become a student of the game. That's what's going to help you move more fluidly. Always conduct yourself in a qualified manner. Remember, you're there to contribute, not to play games.

Setting the boundaries in place in the beginning, is very important. If you don't, you'll forever expend so much energy in trying to re-train people on how to treat you.

When you're in meetings, be clear about what you say and what you stand for so that you can completely get rid of a lot of nonsense. Men communicate differently; learn how they interact so you can keep up.

She Is King

She Is King

Having A Seat At The Table

She Is King

Being able to sit at a table where my voice is heard is incredible. It feels great to contribute my skills and talent to such a powerful organization and group of people. Not just as an owner of a professional basketball team, but with everything that I do. I'm very mindful of how I operate. Having a leadership role isn't just about me; it's not about bragging or boasting; it is making sure that I'm doing this right because I want to make it easy for the young girls coming behind me. Because it was so difficult for me, and it's still difficult for me, and I still deal with lots of stuff every day, I know there's still a lot of work to be done to ensure women get leadership roles based on skills and integrity. There's a tremendous amount of work to be done in the community, and I want to contribute to that work. I want to make sure that I don't slack or cut corners. People are watching me, and I want to give them a great example to follow.

Now, I'm not a women's empowerment guru or anything like that. However, I'm passionate about supporting and mentoring women in high-power positions or women who aspire to level up in their careers. I genuinely want to see more women doing things that not only make them money but make them happy. Women are needed in these spaces but not just because we're eye candy. We're thought-leaders, innovators, visionaries, and the world needs to see that. I'm going to do my part to make sure that it's being shown. It takes nothing for me to lend a listening ear or give some of the wisdom that I've acquired on my journey: I'm simply just lifting another woman. That's what my seat at the table is for anyway, to share my testimony with full transparency that helps other women stay motivated.

You know, there's a lot of power in your testimony and transparency. After speaking with women over the years about what I've gone through and seeing them use it as fuel for their own dream has been rewarding. Seeing them being inspired by my past encouraged me to keep sharing my story, my imperfect story. A lot of people always want to present this perfect story. Well, a perfect story doesn't empower anyone. If anything, it makes them envious. Share your story, raw and uncut, and I bet you, someone's life will be changed.

My seat at the table is essential to me, and I don't take it lightly. I don't hold anything back when I'm mentoring anyone.

One of the things I tell my mentees is to stay in preparation. Preparation brings peace. If you're prepared, then you'll be able to hit almost every shot. You'll be able to maneuver in different spaces. So, prepare yourself for what you want. Study whatever field that you're going into so that you can maneuver as thoroughly as possible. Preparation is the best thing that you could do. Preparation, prayer, and persistence are very crucial.

Empowerment Is Essential

She Is King

I know the word empowerment gets thrown around a lot, especially among women. However, I'm here for it. I also know many women have different definitions, but for me, it's just about transparency and using your story. Without transparency, there's no women's empowerment.

It is essential for women to feel empowered. For me, I think the only true empowerment comes from God. He is the main source of receiving that surge of confidence, strength, and clarity that comes with being connected to Him. You must surround yourself with real, genuine people. It's a lot easier said than done, but it is necessary. Having people who tell you the truth will empower you tremendously because it will give you the level of integrity you'll need in all areas of your life. It will keep you grounded and keep you humble. You'll be able to see where you truly are on your journey.

I found that many people surround themselves with people that feed their ego; most people want fans and not friends. This behavior creates a false sense of empowerment. Therefore, it never works in the end; it is never the real, true sense of empowerment. But I believe, most importantly, that developing your relationship with God, and hearing what He has to say about you, is all that you need to get started.

So, what does it mean to become empowered? Well, for me, it is a matter of getting in a space where I could just be quiet and okay with being by myself. And then, of course, pray, which is just a conversation. Speaking of prayer, I want people to get out of this stigma of making it look like a whole big charade to pray because God is not even like that.

So yeah, you could start by being okay with being with yourself in your quiet time and then adding the conversation with God. There is always a bunch of stuff out there; you can get books and stuff, but I believe the quiet time is where it starts. If you can quiet your mind down, you can manifest anything.

I noticed that when I'm in my feminine energy, I instantly feel empowered. Doing things like going to get my hair done, making sure that my manicures are together, going to a spa, you know, and doing things that require me to focus on myself makes me feel empowered. Giving yourself the attention you need, helps one mentally; it gives a boost of confidence. So many women feel like that's a treat, whereas it really should be normal. So, normalizing luxury and self-care is super important for women. It's a part of showing themselves love, and that trumps everything else in her world.

Ladies, Use Your Voice

If there's one thing I wish I would have done sooner in my career, it's that I wish I had found my voice earlier in my career. Man! I would have avoided some major disappointments. It took me a while, but I'm finally starting to speak up more. I'm going to get more committed to stepping out into the forefront and being more vocal publicly. That's why I'm happy about this book; it pushes me out of my comfort zone regarding just being more vocal, present, and in the forefront. I'm very committed to sharing what it is that I know. And I truly hope that it can help women to be risk-takers, but also to protect themselves. Women need to set themselves up before they step out and do the preparation work. I think people don't think about that when they have the vision and the idea or go into a different industry. There are some things you'll need to prepare for, especially in male-dominated industries.

I won't lie and say it'd be easy standing up for yourself, but it's imperative. As women, we have to set the tone on how men treat us. It starts with not being afraid to speak up. The worst thing they can do is fire you. And guess who has skills and can get another job?

That's right!

The one thing I hope that women reading this book take away is that you are valuable. You are more than your looks, shapes, and clothes. It's a beautiful thing being a woman and possessing sensual power, but let's not use it in the boardroom. Let's keep our minds focused on being leaders, visionaries, and servants. Whether you're in a male-dominated industry or not, honor your womanhood by embracing it and not being afraid to roar.

Learning To Love Giovanni

She Is King

So, when I first started my entrepreneurial journey, I did not understand personal development whatsoever. I just thought I needed to know how to maneuver in the right rooms amongst the right people. I had no clue that the way I treated myself would or could affect how I showed up professionally. When you do not have a proper understanding of who you are, there is a higher chance that you will find yourself in situations that will tarnish your reputation. Too often, women feel the need to sacrifice their integrity and do things or interact with people who mean them no good. Lack of self-love will have you removing your boundaries for love, money, or success. This is why it's important for you to take time and get to know yourself. You must know yourself and love yourself first. It is imperative that you have a sense of self-love, so you won't put up with certain situations, personally or professionally.

While I believe that self-love is about transparency and acceptance, I've realized that you cannot truly love yourself until you've confronted the pain, the flaws, the trauma. From my perspective, you have to go through all those things to get to that point, you know, of true self-love. I don't think there's any self-love until you sit in your pain and reflect on the decisions you've made. Address the elephant in the room. The pain you either received or caused is the change that you will have to confront. Self-love is also changing; you cannot love and stay in your mess as well.

For me, that elephant was the choices that I made with my children. I put my career before them. You know, in the beginning, it all looked like running the streets, chasing gigs. And dealing with a man that I really shouldn't have been dealing with. It looked like having unhealthy relationships.

At some point, I used materialistic things to cope with my pain and made up for when I was away with my kids. It was my therapy. My addiction to shopping was equivalent to someone addicted to alcohol. Like, it didn't matter what store I went in; I was spending my money or someone else's. Anytime I got mad, happy, sad, glad, or whatever, I'd head to the mall or someone's plaza. I wasn't choosey about where or what I'd spend the money on. I could go ball out in the Dollar Tree or Neiman's. It didn't even matter, right? I mean, I did all of this just for the satisfaction and the instant gratification that eased my pain. When I first started, I was clear on what I wanted to do; unfortunately, I sacrificed time with my children to get there. The pain of that coupled with the people around me not understanding my vision fueled my addiction.

Eventually, the addiction burned out, and I was still in pain. So, I had to let go of looking for temporary satisfaction through shopping. I had to learn to just deal with it; I had to learn balance. It was time for me to get real with myself. I had to ask myself the hard question: is this worth it? Learning balance and dealing with my issues head-on has allowed me to be a better mother, friend, daughter, and boss. Your first opportunity in learning how to run a team of people starts in the home: my children taught me that.

I can't exactly pinpoint when I fell in love with myself again, but I realized that I grew as a person. I'd gotten older and just had different experiences that allowed me to see me. I started to trust my mind. I started to see my value in what I was doing, and I realized that I was creating my path. I started separating myself from people that didn't elevate me. I began to stand on my values, my talents, my gifts, and things like that. Of course, coupled with God, I realized a lot of things I accomplished on my own, and not many can do that. So, there's value in that. I didn't necessarily need all of the hoopla to complete the tasks in front of me. That was when I started to shift and change my outlook and my approach. I was striving to be the most capable, not the most visible.

Self-love for me meant finding my voice. It was believing that I could voice out my opinion and change the narrative. To be clear, you do not have to do every single thing; you do not have to take every phone call, and you do not have to take every opportunity. On this self-love journey, you must align yourself with people and opportunity that progresses your vision. Real opportunity will not drain you. Personally, I no longer felt that I have to do this and to do that. And it truly helped me love myself just a little more than I did before.

Surprisingly, having daughters increased the desire to love myself more. I love my sons, but having little girls pushed me to really do my inner work. Leading by example, I establish a foundation for how they will view themselves as women now and in the future. I am pushing to break barriers to make my little girls' journeys easier and for all of the little girls out there.

I'm A Baby Mom… And?

She Is King

It's no secret that I'm a mom of four. It's also no secret that I'm not married. So technically, I'm a single mother, and at times, I'll refer to myself as a baby mom. Can you believe that some women cringe when I say this? Why are women ashamed of being referred to as a baby mom? You have a baby. You're a mom. What's the big deal?

In our society today, people view being called a baby mom as some sort of curse. Although I want to be married, I do not carry the shame of not being married. People love to make women feel as though it's frowned upon to be a single mother, but I feel differently. While most women get embarrassed, I'm unbothered. Some even find it offensive. Not sure why I should be offended by this, but hey, it is what it is. When you're a teen mom, you don't have time or space to be offended by what people say about you because they'll clearly have something to say.

So yeah, I'm not ashamed of being a baby mom. Trust me, I could have been married if I wanted to be, but I'm not, and I am cool with that for now. I don't know. I'm probably lying! But yeah, calling myself a baby mom is more for shock value. You know, people think that when Black women get pregnant, their life is over, and they need to go stand in the welfare line or go to Planned Parenthood. The society makes unmarried Black women feel as if they're worthless for having a child without a husband. It trips me out that when I say that I'm a baby mom, people look at me in disbelief as if they want to ask, "How could you say that about yourself?" And I think it's the saddest thing. Sure, I can be a lot more graceful in how I say it but saying it like that kind of just brings it back to the reality of the situation — the judgment that comes with it. I've decided not to be ashamed about being unmarried or offended by people pointing out the obvious. No Black woman should feel ashamed about having a baby, no matter her age or relationship status. What gets me about this is that a white woman or teen girl would never be judged like this.

For instance, with the show "Teen Mom" on MTV, those girls got glorified for having babies, and they were horrible. None of them were referred to as a baby mom. That word was never used on that show. Without a doubt, I know that's because they were white teen girls. If these were Black, 13-, 14-, 15-year-old teen girls getting pregnant or having multiple babies, they would be dragged for filth. But not the white teen moms. They were superstars. It was never looked at in the way of, "Oh my god, how could you do that?" or "Oh no, your life will be over." No, it wasn't bad at all for the white teen girl to become an unwed mom — it wasn't that at all. But for me, a Black teen girl who gives birth to her first child is reduced to being a baby mom.

Yeah, okay. I'll be that.

I call myself a baby mom because I want the other Black teen moms, whether younger or older, to embrace being the most beautiful thing a woman can be — a mother. Doesn't matter how the baby was brought into this world, he or she is here, and it's a beautiful thing. So, what that you're not married? And hey, you never know, you could be married a year from now. I don't know. What I do know is that I'm going to push the narrative that your life isn't over, and you can still be something, whatever you desire to be despite being a baby mom.

Over time, dealing in this industry, I realized how villainized unwed Black moms are, and it's just wrong. Welcoming the phrase baby mom is a conversation starter. I'd love to change people's narratives on it. I've been kind of practicing this with one of my mentors: he's very, very wealthy. Both of us have these very concrete conversations about life. These days, I try to surround myself with people that I want to emulate. I'm learning that my network has to be on a certain level because of where I'm trying to go. And so, I've even been able to change his perspective on treating unwed mothers and Black women in general. Well, we had to have that conversation because when I got pregnant, he was like, "what, another baby?" And then, once he realized that being pregnant didn't stop my grind, he had to respect it. He even asked me to forgive him for putting those barriers on me without allowing me to still thrive in my position. At the end of the day, you can change the stigma, just as you can change the narrative. Being a wife or even a baby mom does not determine your value. You have to write your own story, just like you're reading mine!

Balancing It All

She Is King

Being a mother and a business owner have definitely been a struggle. The phrase work-life balance is thrown around a lot, and to be honest, I haven't mastered that yet! I think it's something that's you're always going to be working on. Like most women, I sometimes feel the pressure of getting to a certain point in my career. I feel the need to be all things to everyone, and that's just not realistic. It's like, I want to work, I want to create, I want to be a mom and a wife, but when will I do all of this? Twenty-four hours never feels like enough time — I know you can relate. And I've done all the things people recommended. Yeah, I've been inspired by some people, but I don't feel like I've been inspired enough actually to implement a specific strategy into my life.

Can I just be honest with you?

Sometimes I go a little overboard. Okay, most times, I go overboard. What can I say? I'm naturally driven, so I extend myself when I know I should rest. I've been learning, especially with COVID-19; I've been kind of down to prioritize balancing my life more.

There are some things I'll have to say no to, events that I'll have to skip for the sake of spending as much time with the kids as possible or just having a day to myself. It's okay to take a day off and put your cape in the closet. We all have different lives, so I don't want to say what you should do to create balance. I will say: get creative. Find unorthodox ways to make time for your work, family, friends, love life, and most importantly, yourself.

She Is King

Becoming A Boss

She Is King

Someone asked me, "What does being a boss mean to you?"

My answer, "To be honest, you cannot be a boss without being a worker first. I believe there is no true leadership without serving."

I take pride in serving the people around me.

I've learned that being a true boss is a process. In my opinion, a true boss is humble. A boss is someone who doesn't mind doing the work, not necessarily someone who wants to tell other people what to do. I work alongside my employees as if I were in the same position as them. For example, if you were to be present at The Camden Monarch's basketball games, it would be hard to point me out within my staff. I value the work ethic of my staff, and I plan always to mirror their efforts.

I'm always uncomfortable when people refer to me as a "Boss" or a "Boss Chick" because that's not how I view myself. Well, at least not to the standards of social media. I think that social media is misconstruing who a boss is. Number one, bosses work. And from what I've seen, most people who are calling themselves bosses aren't doing much. A lot of times, it frustrates me to see people glamorize being a boss because it's everything but that. And it's unfortunate because it gives people a false sense of what it means to truly be in position. The title is thrown around so loosely. For that reason, I don't refer to myself as a boss. Although technically, I am one, to me, it means nothing. A lot of bosses want to be seen. However, I just want to be impactful. My goal is always to be the most capable, not the most visible.

To be a boss means you understand every aspect of your business. You delegate, you create, you support, and you work. Whether I refer to myself as a boss or not, I'm going to work in any scenario, and that's where I feel most people drop the ball. Once they get to a certain level in their career, they no longer have to put skin in the game. What I want people to know is that titles aren't necessary. It's all about your work ethic. Whether I'm an owner, the CEO, a top executive, or whatever, I always outwork everybody, and I know how to do everyone's job efficiently.

Number two, bosses are always learning. YOU MUST BE A STUDENT OF THE GAME. No one knows it all or can do it all, so you must surround yourself with people you can continuously learn from and grow with. Majority of my employees have gone to pursue their own businesses with the tools and knowledge they acquired while working under me, constantly finding new ways to sharpen their skills and hone their craft. Bosses serve others. They look out for their team, support them, and put them in position to lead. Bosses create other bosses, period. I did not acknowledge myself as a boss until I helped put people in positions to win. Bosses are not swindling their fingers, watching others work their vision. Bosses are in the trenches doing the work.

One of the things I learned early on while becoming a leader is how important ownership is, especially for women. In my experience, I've found that most people focus on being a boss rather than being an owner, and there's a difference.

It's super important for women to own their vision and have something they can claim for themselves, something that they can create or build that mirrors their thoughts and minds. When a woman has ownership, it empowers her; it gives her a sense of self. It definitely did that for me.

Women are always second to men. You rarely see a woman in an ownership role, especially in Corporate America. It's usually led by men, which I think is fine.

However, women need to have something that we can call ours. We need something that we can be proud of, something that we can hold on to, one second.

Becoming an owner has taught me so much about being a woman. I feel like that's part of the reason why I am mentally strong. Being in this position helped me with my sense of self, sense of understanding, and capabilities. It caused me to push myself to step up to the plate and exercise my responsibilities. When you own something, you're responsible for everything. So, it made me operate to my full potential to get something going, and I think it helped. I believe this is a great trait for women to have, which I hope other women strive to become.

She Owns A What?

She Is King

I have to say, taking on the role of an owner of a basketball team was not something I put on my vision board. If someone had told me that I'd even be considered for a role like this, I would have politely laughed them away. Although sports were a huge part of my childhood and teenage years, it wasn't something I was seeking to get into from a business perspective. I didn't look for this opportunity. It basically fell into my lap, and I took it.

My partner, at the time, was working with the ABA, which is the American Basketball Association, and he brought the idea to me. The ABA is the longest-running and largest Basketball League. The NBA actually came from the ABA. So, when he mentioned it, I didn't think much of it. I just thought he was ambitious, but he was serious.

Initially, when we talked about it, I wasn't going to be at the forefront, which was fine with me. I preferred to be in the back, making things happen, so I didn't make a fuss about it. But everybody around me saw the vision first. They all thought that it would be an excellent fit for me. Being that I was a woman, and no other woman had this role, I was a little apprehensive because, you know, I usually play the role that no one ever sees. In public relations, you're always in the background: behind the artists, behind the client or the film or whatever.

And so, I just thought about it: I thought, you know, this would be a good time to step into the more visible role to empower women. It has always been my play, always trying to, you know, encourage a woman or a young girl. And so, I did that. I decided to take a step further into leadership, and more operative roles, you know, more of the CEO role of the ownership. Fortunately, it worked out, but unfortunately, my partner and I split towards the middle of the season. Therefore, I had to take full responsibility. And so, I did, and I'm still doing that.

Now, let me be clear: transitioning into this role was very, very difficult for me. It was grueling. It was something that I'd never done before. Therefore, it took a lot of faith. There were a lot of sleepless nights, a lot of tears. I have to say I didn't have the support I felt I needed at the time. Therefore, it was hard to balance being a mom, run my existing businesses, and learn this new position was very hard. Not only did I not have the support I wanted, but I also didn't have many people believing in me, and that was tough. I didn't realize the importance of having someone in your corner, rooting for you when you feel like giving up. So, I had to believe in myself. I had many moments where I was like, "Girl, wait, you want to do what?" I had to be the one to ask myself since no one else was around to ask me.

When I told people that I would own a professional basketball team, I didn't get the "Oh, that's great"; instead, I got a lot of backlash. I'd hear stuff like, "Oh, I think you need to give yourself more time." "What do you mean by a professional basketball team?" "What do you mean, you're going to bring it to Camden?"

Knowing that people doubted me added more weight to my existing uncertainty. And to be honest, I'm not sure if they doubted me or just didn't fully understand the vision. I believe that people wanted to support me but just didn't know-how. I believe the idea was just too big for some. Although I understand that now, at the time, I only had support from the Lord, my parents, and my closest friend. Eventually, my mentor helped me gain the confidence that I needed so I can do my thing. Once my mind grasped that I had the position, I was ready to do the work.

Now, I mentioned that real bosses do work, and I put in a lot of work because, you know, it was my baby. So, work for me as an owner looked like communicating with employees, overseeing events with the General Manager, managing the concession stand inventory, public relations, you know, all of that stuff that makes the team operate smoothly. Now that I'm settled in my role, I feel a lot more comfortable with the people that are left.

I could go on and on about how I felt during the process, but the feeling I felt when everything came together was just amazing. It became surreal for me. My most memorable moment was the first game. We're sold out, and I just remember standing with the mayor and just taking it all in. I looked out as I received recognition, and I felt proud, just seeing my family and all the faces that were there in support. I vividly remember seeing my father in the owner's box, smiling and cheering for me, with my closest friend standing behind the DJ booth. At that moment, a sense of relief filled inside of me. There was an amazing feeling like, "Wow, you really pushed through." It couldn't have been a more perfect day other than us losing by two points, but it was the most perfect bit.

She Is King

Everyone Can't Go… And That's Okay

She Is King

It's natural to want to take the people you started with to the top. You want to make money with your friends, your family, and your spouse. In essence, I wanted the same. However, what I learned is, when you have a vision, it's yours. You can't get caught up in the people that you started with. See, your vision is a puzzle, right? And your whole goal is for you to be able to put all the puzzle pieces together. And sometimes, the puzzle pieces you start with don't fit. Therefore, you can't get attached to such puzzle pieces. You have to move them out to get a better fit; you must be attached to the vision and the end goal. So that's what I had to learn. And to truly be dedicated to your vision, you'll have to remove some people from your journey, and that's okay.

A lot of times, our instinct wants around us people we feel that we can trust, but sometimes it doesn't work like that. My best lesson on this path is learning to trust God's plan and to trust my heart. My heart has never led me astray. That's a beautiful gift women have. The ability to use our heart and our discernment to make choices that will benefit us — use it.

No one can get to their next level alone. Yes, you need people, but sometimes those people won't look like you. They won't come from the same neighborhood as you. They won't speak, walk, or dress like you. Your blessing won't be attached to a person that even thinks like you. Therefore, you have to be open to walking away from familiar environments to unlock your next level.

Please Hold The Applause

She Is King

Having a humble spirit is the best you can have. I've seen so many people crash and burn because of ego. And I just refuse to be that person. Like, it's not even important to me if people know who I am or what I am. What's more important is that I'm effective and impactful. It's not important that when I come in, people are schmoozing me and all that stuff. Most of the time, I usually stop that, like, you don't have to do that. Remaining approachable allows me to connect with everyone that surrounds me. I want people to be humbler. I do not like fake energy around me: I hate that type of stuff. It wears me out. To be honest, those kinds of stuff stopped me from going to certain places and doing certain things because of what the people there act like.

    I remember one time I was speaking at Drexel University, and I was up there with some other CEOs or whatever. They were all talking about what success looks like. The whole time I sat there, I was just shaking my head, listening to them give these kids mediocre tips to success. When I got up there, and I was like, "Listen, if you don't want to go to school, then stop going to school, and if you don't want to do this, then stop doing this. I know that they're saying XYZ, but I'm the only person up here who owns anything at the end of the day. They still work for somebody." I just had to give those students a different perspective, and they respected it in the end. Now during my speech, they gave a sista the side-eye. Here we are sitting in one of the top schools in the country, and I'm telling the students don't go to school if they don't want to go to school. But hey, it was imperative to keep it as transparent as possible. That's because many of these people, once they get to a certain thing, feel like they have to keep this certain vibe going. And it's just not reality. And I think it paints a different picture for kids or whoever that's aspiring to be in certain places. And I think it's just a load of crap. For me, humility allows me to walk in my truth and share my journey to success in a transparent manner. At the end of the day, your dreams do not always require the traditional steps to achieve them. I believe all you need is God, faith, and hard work, respectfully.

In learning to love myself, I discovered that my power lies within my humility. Sure, other people look at what I do as something powerful, and that's dope. I just don't look at myself like that. I don't feed into it too much because when you start feeding into the influence part, it takes your mind off of who's influencing you. To be frank, I just want to stay focused on what God is telling me to do. NEVER GET CAUGHT UP IN THE HYPE. I try to stay as grounded as possible. I choose to stay grateful for the success I've been blessed with and grounded enough to receive new blessings. I understand that I still have so much stuff to do, so I want to stay in action. But I have to be honest; sometimes, when I have the opportunity to sit back and reflect, I be like, "Wow, girl, you did that!" I don't do that too often because I feel like it'll get me off of my path if I do that. I'll clap for myself at the end.

So, no celebrations for me right now. Please hold the applause.

She Is King

She Is King

Lessons To Becoming A Leader

She Is King

One thing I want you to take away from this chapter is that God has given you everything that you need. He's given you the vision; He's already given you the provision to be able to obtain it; you just have to be obedient, listen, and exercise your tools. That's one of the things that I hold on to, which keeps me away from a place of fear, weary, or self-doubt because I know that I've already been equipped to be able to carry out the mission.

There are so many lessons that I've learned about myself while being in leadership roles. You have to follow the yellow brick road and pick up new talents that will keep you going. Every day is a fight, so you have to exercise your tools. And I think the biggest tool that we have is our tongue. I truly believe in speaking over yourself and speaking life into yourself. I believe in combating anything that may meet you in your day in the morning, whether it's self-doubt or anything. I believe that you can speak what it is that you want to see. For example, if you're not a self-starter, you can speak that into yourself. Stand in the mirror and say out loud, "I am a self-starter. I am efficient." Everything will start lining up with what it is that you put out. Another great lesson I learned about becoming a leader is that it's important to be confident. If you don't believe in yourself and in your abilities, nobody else will, period. People in this day and age are rarely going to vouch for you. So, you need to be your best advocate: you need to be your biggest fan. It's super important that your confidence is there when you walk into a boardroom, or a job interview, or in front of a classroom or group of people. And lastly, a very important lesson I learned is that you need to have the education to keep up. Like, there is nothing wrong with self-teaching. You use your phone all day to look at nonsense. Instead, use it to study and get information about what it is that you're trying to do. We have a brain, so let's use it to grow and evolve in all areas of our lives.

Before I go, I want you to know that even the smallest of progress is progress. Every step you take is closer to your end goal. I want you to know that you're doing enough. Even if you stumble a bit, just keep going. Don't be so hard on yourself. Do not get caught up in the things that you see around you. Know that everybody's journey is different. What God has for you is still yours, just trust His voice and follow the path He has carved out just for you. Remember to be kind with yourself, be gentle with your spirit, and be fair with your heart. Give yourself the grace to mess up and start over... REMEMBER, you can always start over. These are principles that I stand on because they've really helped me to shift my thinking and to just shift my life. And I believe that if I continue to do it, I will definitely be where I want to be — and so will you.

She Is King

About the Author

Giovanni Thompson is a young fiery powerhouse, who is the CEO of the Camden Monarchs and the owner of GioGlobal Management. With over 10 years of experience in music & entertainment, she has vowed to use her platform to inspire & propel young girls.

www.ingramcontent.com/pod-product-compliance
Lightning Source LLC
Chambersburg PA
CBHW031155160426